Copyright © 2018 by Allyson M. Goode

All rights reserved. This book or any portion thereof may not be reproduced or used in any manner whatsoever without the express written permission of the publisher except for the use of brief quotations in a book review.

Printed in the United States of America

First Printing, 2018

ISBN 9781728808246

She Overcame is a memoir of my life experiences, reflections, prayers, and conversations I've had in the last few years. Each of the experiences I've written about have, in some way, shaped who I am and who I am becoming as a Christian black woman of the millennial generation. The accounts in this book are told through transparent lenses in order to hopefully help someone else overcome their deepest and strongest hurts. This book is inspired by my late mother's, Vanessa Mitchell Goode, written testimony, "Then Sings My Soul" in the book, "Through It All: Wisdom of The Ages", an anthology of seasoned wisdom by Grace Church International's Seasoned with Grace Seniors Ministry. My mother's story impacted me because first, I read it almost a year after she passed, and second because I realized how important it is to share how God uses our human experiences for divine glory. My scripture of reflection, and often correction, comes from The Bible in 2 Corinthians 12:9-10,

"And he said unto me, My grace is sufficient for thee: for my strength is made perfect in weakness. Most gladly therefore will I rather glory in my infirmities, that the power of Christ may rest upon me. Therefore I take pleasure in infirmities, in reproaches, in necessities, in persecutions, in distresses for Christ's sake: for when I am weak, then I am strong."

My prayer is that this book shed light in darkness, encourage strength in weakness, inspire joy in the time of sorrow, bring peace in situations of unrest, promote love when there are feelings of hate, be a victory for the defeated, tell of courage when it's easier to be fearful, and inspire the uninspired.

I dedicate this book to Vanessa Goode, Gregory Goode, Sr, Gregory Goode, II, Lydia Reneé Goode, and my winning support system made up of family and my closest friends.

Superwoman

Empty Cup

ReEvaluation

Change

Get Ready

Letter to Myself

Mama's Girl

Beginning of Purpose

Just Jump

Coach Goode

My Testimony

Faith

The Journey

Shine

Forgiveness

Overcome

SUPERWOMAN

Romans 8:18 -I consider that our present sufferings are not worth comparing with the glory that will be revealed in us.

I stood over her lifeless body.
I called her "sister".
I whispered her name.
Hoping that she'd wake up at the sound of my voice as she had done before.
I tried to shake her.
But nothing changed.
She had taken her last breath before I could come to her side.

I cried over her still warm body.
Hoping that it was all a nightmare.
Praying that this was not happening and believing we could all go home together as we had done before.
I tried to pinch myself.
But I didn't come out of it.
Life as I knew it would never again be.

I watched her body lay there in sheets
Wondering how hard she fought.
Apologizing silently for not being there to fight with her.
Knowing that going home didn't mean what it meant before.
I wept myself tired.
but I could not sleep that night.
My heart shattered into a million pieces.

I prayed next to my sister's body.
Asking God to make sense of it all.
Demanding that He give me the strength to live with a broken heart.
Begging Him to mend it so I could go on like I was going on before.
I wanted to numb the pain.
But nothing seemed to do the trick.
I'll never forget that night.

It was almost midnight, I was in bed asleep after a long day at work and dinner with my girl friends. My phone rang, and it was my father calling from the hospital. I answered it, figuring it had to be important because it was late. The night before my sister was very sick and weak. She was not doing well, so my parents had to call the paramedics to come assess the issue and help. I remember that night, seeing the fear in Lydia's eyes as she said, "Allyson, I'm not going to die am I?" Being the big sister, and helping her stay calm, I said, "No girl, you're fine! Mom and Dad called the paramedics to come. You'll be okay." Lydia had been sick before, even sick to the point of calling 911, but I felt something different this time around. The next night came, Lydia had been in the hospital for almost 24 hours. I didn't make it over to the hospital that day, but I told my mom I'd promise to come the next day if she wasn't home yet. I answered my dad's call, and I heard him say, "Allyson, you and Greg need to come to the hospital. Lydia coded again." In my mind, I said "Again?", but in reality I said, "Okay, we're on the way." I jumped out of bed to run in the living room to tell Greg. "Greg, Dad said Lydia coded. We're going to the hospital, let's go! He hurried and got dressed, and I grabbed my hoodie, threw on some sweats, put on my slides, snatched the keys, and jetted out the door. I remember driving up the road saying, "Lydia, hold on! We're coming! We're coming!" Greg and I jumped out the car, walked into the building to sign in as a guest of a patient. As soon as we got upstairs, we met our parents in a separate room, and we both said, "Where is she?" Then the doctor escorted the four of us to Lydia's room. As we walked in, several doctors were leaving. There was a curtain barricading the section we walked into, but I could still see Lydia in the bed. The lead doctor said, "I'm sorry. We tried everything we could. She did not make it." Immediately, the sounds of weeping from my parents, my brother, and me filled the small room. It was unreal. I felt my heart get heavy as it broke trying to understand the reality of what we were just told. Throughout the night, family and close friends came to be with us. We cried, we prayed, and we hugged one another. We had to begin making difficult phone calls, and we had to begin making funeral arrangements for my sister, Lydia.

I never knew what strength really was until I became my weakest. October 1, 2015 at 12:10am my life changed forever. However, at the moment, I didn't know how. With the news that Lydia had died from a kidney infection, I was met with a circumstance that I could not control or have any input. I left the hospital that night faced with the difficult task of grieving the death of Lydia. I quickly learned how to hide my emotions in front of people, to cry and release privately. There were things that needed to be done, and I could not do them if I was torn apart or isolated. Over the course of the next several days, I did not go to work.

Our home was a revolving door of family, friends, coworkers, church members, and others who wanted to pay their respects to our family. I spent hours of each day leading up to the funeral listening to others tell stories of how they remember when my siblings and I were young children. I was constantly answering questions of "what happened?" or listening to unsolicited advice on how to cope with loss. I was exhausted!

The day of the funeral service came quickly. My sister's friends suggested that we wear purple, which was Lydia's favorite color. Everyone was dressed nicely, family and friends from all over and from different chapters of Lydia's life filled the sanctuary to celebrate her. I vividly remember walking in the church holding Greg's arm, and I just broke. Seeing my baby sister in that casket tore me down to my core. I felt it in my heart so heavily in that moment. I felt like a ton of bricks were in my chest as I cried uncontrollably. It was a real and vulnerable moment for me. The service was beautiful and uplifting. I was proudly overwhelmed by the number of people who showed up to say their goodbyes to Lydia.

After the funeral, family and friends returned to their hometowns and back to their regular lives. The house began to experience less visitor traffic, and the phones were ringing much less than the week before. I spent the remaining days of the week hanging out with friends in attempt to surround myself with people who I knew cared about me and could lift my spirits.

I went back to work after being away for ten days. When I got back to work, I was showered with love and support from my colleagues and my students. It was October, which meant it was also time to begin preparations for basketball season. Because I was the head coach, I had to quickly get back into the swing of things. I just wanted things to be as normal as possible at work because home life had been a drag since losing my sister. I was ready to be back because teaching all day and coaching all evening was much better than sitting at home crying my eyes out. Working kept me distracted. I had learned once again how to publicly mask my feelings in order to show others that I was okay. I spent my weekends out of town and partying with my friends. It was homecoming for our college alma mater, so we drove down to tailgate and party with our college friend group. The entire time I was missing my sister, but I wanted things to be normal so I carried on partying like nothing was wrong. I went out of state the following weekend, just to get out of Georgia altogether because everything, and I mean everything, reminded me of my sister. That was a breath of fresh air, but it didn't mend my broken heart. It didn't even really offer any significant comfort. The last weekend of the month, I went out to a Halloween party. I had made up my mind that I had a very tough month and this night of partying and fun would be the thing that got me back on my rocker and back to my normal life. I was so wrong, again. The night was fun, and I had a great time, but I still had not given any significant attention or time to recognize my feelings about losing my only sister. I had become real good about not showing my hurt. Social media had no idea, and I was constantly flooded with messages of "you're so strong," "I don't know how you do it," "take care of Mom and Dad!" However, I was very weak, I had no idea how I was doing it either, and I really needed to be taking care of myself. I found myself wearing the superwoman cape that was put on me by others. I accepted a false sense of strength, when I was ultimately weak. I was becoming what I thought I was supposed to be, and I felt that if I could fake it long enough, it would soon be real for me.

At the end of October, I had an encounter with someone who wanted to speak to me. Several days before I got a call and a voicemail message from an unknown number. The message was saying that the particular person was just thinking of me, reaching out to me, and to give her a call back. I ignored it because I was over the generic phone calls of condolences from people who really didn't know me. Eventually I saw the person face to face to let her know that I got her voicemail. Also, that I had not called her back due to being busy. That was a lie, but it would've been rude to tell the truth. She said something different to me than what others had been saying. We briefly talked about how we were similar in that we were both older sisters and some other things. At the end of the conversation, she told me to call her if I needed to talk. I felt her genuineness, but I didn't think I needed to talk.

In my mind, I was holding it together fairly well for myself. I had my cape on, and I was superwoman.

EMPTY CUP

Proverbs 3:5-6 Trust in the Lord with all your heart and lean not on your own understanding; in all your ways submit to him, and he will make your paths straight.

It was a Thursday, and I was at work. I went through the day, teaching as usual. All of a sudden, I felt overwhelmingly exhausted. I wanted to cry immediately, but I had a classroom full of children. I knew my planning period was coming up in a few, so I was able to suppress my feelings a little longer. A few moments later, I walked the children to their specials and returned to my classroom. I shut my classroom door, sat at my desk, and began to cry. In all honesty, I had no idea why I was crying. Or I knew, but it was so much, I didn't even focus on the why. I just knew I didn't feel too great. The passing of my sister was still so fresh, my aunt's funeral was the day before, I was busting my tail to bring my grades up my first semester of graduate school, I was head coach for the girls' basketball team, and I was a teacher. It was all beginning to weigh heavy on me. I sent a text to someone who I didn't really know too well, but who I felt could help me through this moment. The text said, "I'm overwhelmed." A few minutes after I sent the text, my phone rang, and I answered it. The two hour conversation brought about things that I had not admitted to anyone else, and also things about myself and my situation that I had not yet realized. The first thing was that I had not allowed myself time and space to really take in the events of the previous 6 weeks. In a six week time span, my sister unexpectedly passed away from a kidney infection, and both my uncle and aunt passed away due to the spread of cancer. I'd only taken a week off of work to help my family plan my sister's service. After that, I still went back to work, I began the demanding basketball season, I never had a pause in my graduate courses, and I was trying to take care of my family. The weight I felt was from the load I was carrying. I was not properly taking care of myself, so I had become exhausted and overwhelmed.

I was encouraged to spend the coming break dealing and focusing on myself. I was also charged to give myself time to reflect, meditate, pray, and re-energize for the journey of grieving and moving forward.

The second aspect of this particular conversation that brought things to light was my feelings of guilt. I felt guilty when my sister passed away. I felt like I should've been there when I wasn't. I held off on visiting the hospital to go out to eat with my friends. I promised that I would come the next day, but there was no next day. I don't know, but for a while, I felt like my presence could have made a difference in whether she lived or not. At the time, that's how I felt. I was upset with myself, but I never told anyone I felt guilty for not being there because everyone was going to tell me it wasn't my fault. I knew it wasn't my fault, I knew there was nothing I could have done. Taking the blame, putting some guilt on myself, allowed me to deal inwardly instead of projecting it onto someone else, including God. I felt I could manage the guilt better than I could articulate my misunderstanding of why she had to pass away.

Along with feelings of guilt, I felt jealousy. Around the time my sister was hospitalized, so was my aunt. Lydia passed away after a day in the hospital, and all the while we were planning her funeral, my aunt was diagnosed with terminal cancer. The weeks after Lydia's funeral consisted of the entire family going to the hospital where my aunt was to sit and visit with her for hours. Whenever my mom wanted to, I drove her to the hospital to see my aunt, her sister. After several weeks in the hospital, my aunt was taken home to be made comfortable in her transition. We'd go visit her often, sit with her, talk to her, and just spend quality time. After my aunt passed, my family, once again, got together to celebrate her life. I was sad, I was hurt, and I was tired, I felt like I'd run out of tears because so much was happening in such a short period of time. Through all of those emotions, I was jealous. I was jealous of my mother because she had a chance to say goodbye to her sister, I didn't. I was jealous of my older cousins because in dealing with immediate death, they had spouses and children to hold and comfort them. I felt jealous because it seemed as if everyone around me could be vulnerable and weak, but I couldn't. I felt like I had to quickly pick up the pieces that had been broken and try to put them back together, while everyone else had the time and supports to just take in the fact that pieces have been broken. I was jealous that I was wearing the cape and nobody else.

The conversation, which was more than the few things I've shared, allowed me see how I was beating myself up while I was already down. It allowed me to see that I was putting myself in the driver's seat of a vehicle that had no gas in the tank. It allowed me to see that I was not doing myself or anybody else any good by not taking care of myself. Looking back, I was able to understand that the exhaustion and feeling of being overwhelmed was my "come to Jesus" moment. That day, after the tears, the confessions, the realizations, and the words of advice and comfort, I realized that I needed God to step in and help me get through. I had been pouring from an empty cup, when all I had to do was ask God to fill my cup. For myself, I needed love, comforting, encouragement, rest, understanding, security, and peace. I needed the time to grieve.

That day, I made a decision. It wasn't long, it wasn't extravagant, it didn't even require much. I made a decision to take care of myself emotionally and spiritually. I knew that would be the only way for me to overcome these feelings I was experiencing. Over the next week, I went on vacation. I spent much of my vacation meditating, praying, thinking, planning, isolating, writing, and just refreshing myself for the journey ahead. I asked God for peace and clarity. He told me to walk with Him and He would give me whatever I needed whenever I needed it.

RE-EVALUATION

2 Corinthians 5:17- Therefore, if anyone is in Christ, the new creation has come:The old has gone, the new is here!

"The only real thought that comes to my head is, How is this my life now? I have a hard time understanding, or trying to understand how a year that began so well and positive could become the worst year of my life. I don't understand how life can literally take you from 100 to 0 without warning or a gradual process. I have come to find that there is no blueprint to life. There is no "How to" guide when dealing and going through. People keep telling me I am doing well considering what I am going through. The truth is I am still in a state of shock and disbelief. I do not know how to grieve the loss of my sister and live my life as though it doesn't affect me. Everyday is something new. A new memory, a new emotion, a new smile, and I never know how okay I will be from day to day, sometimes hour to hour. My friends don't know it but I am grateful for each "how are you today?" or "I'm here for you, Ally". The simplest of things brighten my day and spirits."

Excerpt from Journal entry 11/29/2015

One thing I learned, as I began to discover myself, was that change within you doesn't necessarily translate in to change within others. I felt like I was going through a transformation, but the world around me stayed the same. It was difficult to deal with at first. I saw life differently. My view on life, relationships, career, and my spiritual life was on a different level. Many people around me didn't even realize it. I was stressing myself out worried about hurting others' feelings, even if they were the ones who already hurt me. I began to see that at this new level, everyone was not invited. I had no clue the major changes in my relationships that would occur in the coming months. There was some shaking happening, that would soon result in some shifts and changes. I recognized the changes, and I began to re-evaluate my relationships. I asked God to give me the wisdom to let people go who were not good for where He was taking me. Tough thing to ask of God. I had to learn to not get stuck in familiarity. All of this led to me sitting down and really thinking about the type of person I want to be for others and the type of person I want others to be for me. In doing this, it was clear what was important to me. It also showed me what I believed would help me the most in this difficult time in my life. Overcoming a change that is mostly within is not easy. It required hard realizations about myself and the people around me. It required honest conversations with my friends and family. In the end, the goal was to make sure that I had the people around me that were helpful to my emotions.

CHANGE

Psalm 119:105 Your word is a lamp for my feet, a light on my path.

"Dear Heavenly Father,

This burden that I carry is too heavy. I have tried to carry alone, but I can't. The emotions of myself and the emotions of others are weighing me down. I need you. I need you to lift the burdens I am carrying. I have realized that if I continue to try to do this on my own, I will be stunted. I need you to continue to cover me in your love and guidance. I do believe that nothing is impossible for you, and that includes healing me and my family from this hurt we feel...Give us the grace to keep living..."

Excerpt from journal entry 12/19/2015

This journey to finding and building myself had its challenges. I knew that one day my life would change. However, I never imagined that it would happen the way it did, nor take the time that it did. I am not perfect, but I felt the transformation that took place within me. I am not going to lie, it scared me! Becoming someone who I am learning while also introducing others to that someone made me nervous. I realized that my life changed. I changed, but change wasn't happening to everyone else. I believe through this period of time, God continued to reveal who should remain in my life. I do know that there are seasons, but I was hurt when those seasons ended. I often wondered why I have a good heart. I love making others laugh and smile, I love giving and sharing, and I love how it feels to be in a good space. I felt that my heart is so good that it couldn't take the bad. For some time, I felt that when I was down and lonely, I had to question who I could count on to make me smile, laugh, and pour into me the way I did for others. My continuous prayer as I entered 2016 was for God to place people in my life who will pour into me, and not always take. I also prayed that He would give me the wisdom to tell me who those people are. Going forward, blind to the future, I prayed and made clear what I needed in order to overcome my feelings, my fears, my relationships, and my life's circumstances. Prayer had become my tool. I felt like God wanted my attention, and He wanted me to verbally acknowledge that the lightbulb had come on and acknowledge that I needed His intervention in my life. Overcoming my personal selfishness, my I got this under control, let me get this myself attitude was only possible for me through my sincere and desperate prayers.

GET READY

John 14:27 Peace I leave with you; my peace I give you. I do not give to you as the world gives. Do not let your hearts be troubled and do not be afraid.

I walked in the door after work, and my parents were in the living room watching television. My mother had a doctor's visit that day because she was having severe headaches and was uncertain about the cause. Also, it was time for her to continue chemotherapy since she was ready after taking a break after Lydia and my Aunt Samora passed away. I asked my parents how the doctor's visit went. My mom turned to look at me, then she turned to my dad. My dad said, "Do you want me to tell her?" I panicked, and said, "Tell me what? Just tell me!" My mom looked at me and said, "I'm done with chemo, Allyson. I don't want to have chemotherapy anymore. I'm tired. I don't like how it makes me feel. I don't want to go through that anymore." I dropped my eyes slightly. I did not want to cry because I did not want her to feel any guilt or any unease about her decision to discontinue treatment. I gathered myself in seconds, and replied, "Okay, Mom. It's your health. Whatever you decide, we are here to support you." My mother asked me if I wanted to know how much time the doctor said she had to live. I insisted that I didn't want to know, but she told me anyway. My mother said, "If I only have six months, I want the best quality of life I can have. I can't have an unrestricted life if I'm sick from chemo treatments. I agreed, and offered my support of her decision. It wasn't the first time we had the "I'm terminal" conversation. Just a few years prior, Mom found out she had inoperable tumors in her lungs. We talked about her quality of life then. This was much different. In addition to cancer spreading throughout her body, she was grieving the deaths of her youngest daughter, her brother, and her only living sister. I couldn't take anymore of the conversation. I immediately took my bag and coat to my room, then left out for some fresh air. I went to my car and cried. I sat there thinking that I could not lose my mom. I was not ready. I didn't feel ready. I needed my mom around for a long time. Six months was not enough time. We had plans for the future that extended far beyond six months. That night was hard for me. I had support, and shared with a couple of confidants. My mother told me not to tell anyone about it, not even our family. So, not only was she very sick, she wanted to keep it a secret from those closest to us. That made it much more difficult. That night after I gathered myself, I went to talk to my mom privately. She told me that my dad, my brother, and I would be okay. She told me to make sure my cousins were okay, and that I was about that time she let God take her home. Words cannot describe how strong I tried to be while listening to her tell me that she was ready. I did not want to be selfish because I watched the pain she had gone through over the past four years. I had to be strong for her. I didn't see my mom cry much over my life. That night she was vulnerable with me, and she cried to me. My mom tried chemotherapy one more time after that, even though she said she wouldn't. That last time was her last time accepting treatment.

A couple weeks after the conversation about the state of my mom's health, I took a couple days off work to stay home and take care of my mother while my father was out of town. The few days I stayed home with her, I cooked her breakfast and lunch. I also made her famous banana nut bread. She couldn't eat all of it, but she had a little taste of it and said, "This is good, Allyson!" That meant a lot to me because I'm not the best cook in the family. We binge watched a series that we both enjoyed. We shared jokes, we debated about our predictions during the show, and we enjoyed time together. We had a couple mishaps during the day, but we were able to laugh about it later. It was a great couple of days spent together. As sad as I felt on the inside knowing that I was going to eventually lose my mother within the year, I learned something those two days. I learned to enjoy the good moments. In the good moments, I genuinely saw the joys of life. No matter how small or big. I saw the importance of taking the time to see the good in being okay in that particular moment. I learned to smile when I'm happy, and laugh when it's funny. God didn't limit our smiles, so we shouldn't be afraid to use them. The good moments spent with my mother possessed the laughter that cleansed any negativity or toxic feelings I had. In those moments I was able to see what contributions others can make to my happiness and well being. I didn't take much, or anything too complex. A person who can genuinely make your heart smile is a person to have around. The feeling of being happy, enjoying the present, laughing, and being cheerful is amazing, and is a lighter load than the one we would otherwise be carrying if it weren't for a smile.

I believe God allows us to have these epiphanies and bask in these good moments. When moments are bad, we carry these good memories, the smiles, the laughs, and the good emotion deep in our hearts to help get us through the bad moments. I've learned that good moments exist if I let them happen. I learned to be vulnerable. I allowed myself to create good moments, recognize good moments, and just thank God good moments exist.

My story of overcoming is about peace, joy, and courage. I could have spent the time with my mother sad, in tears, being worried, acting fearfully, or thinking with a pessimistic attitude. My friend told me to take emotional cues from my mother. This meant that as long as my mom was in good spirits, I could pull myself together and be in good spirits as well. After all, it was her fight. This didn't mean I didn't have feelings of sadness, but it meant that I was cleared to be fine if my mom was fine. I put my trust in God, put my worries aside, and enjoyed the moments. The good moments. I made a deposit of smiles for the days I would need to cry. I overcame the vicissitudes of life with a smile, laughter, and enjoying the good moments.

LETTER TO MYSELF

Allyson,

I'm very proud of you. The things you have set in your heart are nothing short of admirable The way you have carried yourself through what can be defined as the toughest times of your life show your strength. Your strength is a testament to God's strength. I see you every morning, you wake up, and you go to work each day. You recognize the impact you have on the kids you teach and mentor, and you hold yourself accountable for being there when you can. At a time when it was easy for you to give up, you continued. When it was easier to shut everyone out, you welcomed love. You put your ego aside and accepted the love and guidance you needed. The relationships you have, you have molded them into relationships that are blessings and not burdens. You have reconnected with God and allowed yourself to become more aligned with the purpose He has for you. The visions you have in your heart now have room to make manifest because you have grown and matured in faith. Trusting God is the hardest thing to do when your world seems like it is crashing down, but the peace of mind is in Him, your security and stability is in Him. You have shown your faith in that everything that happens is for your good. I just wanted to tell you that you are beautiful, you are amazing, you are strong, you are brave, you love, you care, you trust, you discern, you believe, you guide, you share, you encourage, you are intelligent, honest, trustworthy, you are open to learning.

I know that it's hard. I know that sometimes you worry about what's next, just keep moving. Just keep pressing on, keep believing in God, keep trusting that you will be okay. You are having this experience for a purpose. People are watching you and seeing you as an example of how to handle what is tough. Feel your feels, be human. At the end of it all, make sure you get up, dust off your pants, and keep going.

I love you.

Excerpt journal entry 03/30/2016

MAMA'S GIRL

Proverbs 31:25-31
She is clothed with strength and dignity;
she can laugh at the days to come.
She speaks with wisdom,
and faithful instruction is on her tongue.
She watches over the affairs of her household
and does not eat the bread of idleness.
Her children arise and call her blessed;
her husband also, and he praises her:
"Many women do noble things,
but you surpass them all."
Charm is deceptive, and beauty is fleeting;
but a woman who fears the Lord is to be praised.
Honor her for all that her hands have done,
and let her works bring her praise at the city gate.

Dear Mom,

   I'm sad that you are gone, but I'm glad that you are still here. Every time I look at myself, I see you. Every time I listen to myself, I hear you. I am the woman I am today because of you. The daughter I am is because I saw the daughter you were to your parents and parental figures. The sister I am today is because I watched how you were to your siblings. The friend I am is because I watched how you were with your friends. Because of you I have no fear in following my dreams and taking risks. The faith in Christ that I have today is because I saw the faith you had. You were a great mother, and I someday hope to be a great mother like you. I can't imagine how my life will be without you here to give me advice and cheer me on, but I hold in my heart the things you have told me and the things you have shown me in the 25 years of my life. I told you that I would be okay when you go on to be with the Lord. I am okay. I will be okay. The tears I cry are because I understand. I asked the Lord to be my strength, and He hasn't let me down. I am strong even when I am weak because of the Lord. As I continue living, I can only pray to continue to make you proud. I will not give up, but persevere as you have taught me. It will be tough, but if I am my mother's daughter, I will make it. I'm glad you are at peace and no longer suffering. I am at peace knowing that you knew the Lord, and you left a legacy of positive impact on thousands of people. I want to be like you when I grow up.

You are my hero, and I will miss you forever. I will love you forever. I will miss you telling me to be safe and have fun. I will miss you asking if it's me walking in the door. I will miss you calling me and telling me to bring you back a soda from the store. I will miss you across the bench from me during basketball season. I will miss you helping me set up my classroom and giving me professional advice. I will miss you rubbing my hair. I will miss driving you around. I will miss your laughter. I will miss you holding my hand in church. I will miss my mama. I will miss my mom. I will be okay because I now have another angel who is watching me.

Your Little Girl.

"Mother's Day in 2016 was not my favorite day of the year. It wasn't a bad day, but it was a day that I needed to figure out how I would deal. This particular Mother's Day, I chose to look on the bright side. I was hurt because I missed her dearly. However, through the hurt I was able to smile. I smiled because my mother knew the importance of a village. She allowed other women to be in my life and make motherly impacts on my life. I'd like to think that she realized that the work of a mother is to do her best to raise me and guide me, as well as to welcome other trusted women to pour into my life. Because of her, I have been touched and cared for by women who love me in ways that mothers love their own children. I have one mom, and although she isn't here anymore, she lives in those women she allowed to be in my life. I could be sad and feel pain in my heart, but I could also be happy and at peace because I am still loved by mother figures. On that Mother's Day, the first without my mom being alive, I chose smiles over tears, laughter over anger, fellowship over isolation all because the love of my mother, Vanessa, did not die with her flesh, but I recognize that love lives on in the love shown to me by many."

Journal excerpt from Mother's Day 05/08/2016

BEGINNING OF PURPOSE

Philippians 2:13 for it is God who works in you to will and to act in order to fulfill his good purpose.

"After getting the news on Friday about the camp, I felt set back. I felt like I failed, I felt like I let myself down. I didn't know what to do or say because of circumstances beyond my control. I cried and said nothing good that is this big ever happens to me. I was extremely upset, and didn't tell anyone except Coach Best Friend. I felt like I was just over it, and didn't even want to press it anymore. I really felt depressed. I came home, cleaned, and cried. I tried to take a nap, and that didn't work. I had things to do, so I put my thoughts of sadness and pity away.

After the weekend was over, I was listening to this song, and the lyrics are "Your ways are higher, your thoughts are wilder", and I was like YES! THIS! It instantly took me back a couple days to a sermon my friend preached. One thing she said that resonated with me was that being kept back isn't a bad thing. This whole situation is just the set up for a blessing in a way that I couldn't imagine for myself. It was just up to me to have faith that what is for me will happen. I have to continue to have faith in what God is going to do for me. God wanted me to have those blessings that were above what my mind could fathom. I had to trust that it's the same spirit that has come over me before that will come through again."

I wrote that journal entry on the 1st of June in 2016. On the 2nd of June, I began writing up a plan to begin my own organization to host my own basketball camps and mentor group. I drew from my experiences and what I felt in my heart I was led to do initially. After a month or so, I realized my plan was too small. I went back to the drawing board , and I visioned bigger things. I gained some inspiration from my sister, Lydia's experiences as a cheerleader. Then I had this idea of a sports program for girls, not just for basketball, but for cheerleader and other sports and athletic activities. Over the next couple of months, God would drop these nuggets into me that would help me craft the big picture and smaller supporting details of my sports academy. I did the research, and took the necessary steps to get officially incorporated under the State of Georgia. Over the next several months, I wrote ideas, made plans, polled people's opinions, had a logo made, and also made some equipment investments for the program.

I overcame a set back, by seeing the glass half full. From an initial standpoint, I failed at not being able to host a basketball camp. After taking a step back, and realizing that bigger and better would come, I was able to listen to God and strategically begin making my dreams come true. I only wanted a basketball camp, but my thinking was too small, so rejection was necessary. Looking at failure as an opportunity to do something better, bigger, and God's purpose driven was the catalyst for me overcoming this set back.

JUST JUMP!

Philippians 4:13 I can do all this through him who gives me strength.

I'd been thinking about it for some months. I did enough research to not confuse or discourage me. I consulted some confidants about the matter, and I even prayed about it. I felt it was time for me to move out of my parents' home and get my own place. I remember vividly the night I was 100% certain that this is what I needed to do. I was at an outdoor worship session, and there came a time where we just partnered up and prayed with one another. I was asked my prayer request, and I said, "Direction." I didn't expound on what I meant because I wasn't certain myself. I just knew that I needed some direction for the next chapter in my life. So we prayed. It was like this person knew exactly what I meant without me saying much. I knew it was the Holy Spirit confirming what I needed to do going forward and where I needed to go. That weekend I found me a place to move to, and I began the process of applying for an apartment. Over the next few weeks, I kept it to myself that I was getting ready to move. I only chose to talk about it with a couple of my confidants. I also didn't want to get my hopes up for everything not work out the way I was planning. Time went by, and I hadn't heard anything back from the management office. So one November Sunday afternoon, I drove over to the place to follow up in person. At the time, I found out that I was approved for a place and could set a move in date. I did just that. I sat on that information for a couple weeks, then I decided to share with my family that I was moving out. I was nervous because I didn't know what type of reactions to expect. I was a very independent person, but for some reason, I felt as if my family wouldn't see that and think that I still wasn't ready for the responsibility of living on my own. I was wrong. My cousins were very receptive and understanding of my choice. They offered to help me with whatever I needed. They also expressed how proud they were of me finally growing into my own and being able to do well for myself. My father, understandably, was not as receptive to finding out that I was officially leaving the nest. He didn't immediately see the need for me to leave home.

When I had that conversation with my dad, I realized that I was going to move out regardless of what anyone else thought. However, I needed to sit back and think on why there was a need for me to move on my own. First, I hit a wall. Metaphorically, I hit a wall that was halting my growth as a woman who needed to become more independent and grow more towards the person I eventually wanted to be. Second, time had passed where taking care of others after the passing of my sister and mother was now taking a toll on my emotional well being. Moving out would allow me the personal time and space to focus on my own grieving process and take care of myself. I owed it to myself to make the necessary moves and sacrifices in order to gain a peace of mind.

The day I was set to move in came. I took off work for the day, then I went to the managing office to sign some last minute papers and to get my keys. At the time, all I had to my name was a television, a dresser, a bed frame (still in the box), my clothes and shoes, my school books, all of my late sister's things that would fit in my Nissan Sentra, and a couple thousand dollars that would easily become a couple hundred after fees and deposits were paid. I did a last walk through inspection of the place, and I received the keys to my new place. I would describe my feelings as ecstatic, overjoyed, nervous, terrified, but overall happy. After the inspector left, I got in my car and hurried to the nearest store to pick up something. Some oil. From a child, I always remembered my parents having a bottle of extra virgin olive oil in the China cabinet. Anytime we'd pray as a family, pray individually, pray over things, other people, or just to bless things, my parents pulled the oil out. Just like it was done at church. When I returned to my new apartment, I was alone and the place was completely unfurnished. I began to pray. In that moment I thanked God for the courage He gave me to do something for myself of such great impact. I thanked God for placing encouragers in my life, who repeatedly told me that I wouldn't be alone, and helped see me through the process. I walked around and anointed my new place with oil as I prayed for safety, comfort, peace, and love. I prayed to God that he'd supply every need of mine concerning having a place of my own. I spent about 10 minutes crying out to God for Him to fill this place with His presence, and expressing my gratitude for all He was doing in my life at the time. I was overwhelmed.

I overcame fear of the unexpected. For several months, I allowed comfort to outweigh my need for peace and comfort. I had to learn to trust that what I was doing would work out because me moving out was a part of God's plan to heal me from all that had hurt me. I had to learn to jump, even when I was afraid. I had to learn to be honest and lean on my support systems. I overcame all that I was in order to step in the direction of who I was to become.

"COACH GOODE"

Proverbs 4:18 The path of the righteous is like the morning sun, shining ever brighter till the full light of day.

There's a term that many of us connected to basketball use, "ball is life." The term means different things depending on who says it and whatever context in which they use it. For some, it means basketball is their top priority, for others it could mean that basketball is their lifestyle, and for some it may even mean that the ways of life are the same as the ways of the game. However, to me, it means neither of these. The phrase, "ball is life" is my reminder of what hoop did for me in my life. It speaks to my experiences, my strengths, my weaknesses, my passions, my influence, my safe space, and it speaks to how I had to overcome several obstacles in my life. I'm often reminded of where I came from, who I came with, where I am now, and where I am going when I think of ball is life.

"Think about what you hope to get out of high school. Be here with a purpose to learn and to grow." Those were words spoken to my homeroom class in 9th grade by our homeroom teacher. Mr. Bradley was giving us some advice and motivation about high school. On the first day of school, I knew that I was planning on becoming one of the top basketball players in my class and hoping to win several championships as a player at my high school. My purpose of going to school each day was to learn and play ball, everything else was extra. Basketball was my number one passion, it was my plan to gain popularity, it was how I planned to go to college , and make a living. I played on the team ninth through eleventh grade. In twelfth grade, my life changed. For the first time in 6 years, I had been cut from the team and was no longer in a position to make my dreams of playing college ball, or professional ball, come true. Being cut from the basketball team changed the way I viewed my passions, people around me, and my future. The impact this event had on my life had not become evident, or even very significant until years later. Before basketball team tryouts my 12th grade year, I spent the fall at conditioning with the other girls who had been on the team in the previous years. Also, there were girls who were new to the school. Every day of the week we would run the cross country loop, the track, and lift weights in the weight room. Due to my summer job, I did not attend summer workouts or play on the summer league team. I knew that me missing out during the summer affected my body, so I had to work extremely hard to get in shape like the other girls. Being a 12th grade varsity player meant so much to me, and I was excited to play basketball that year. Every senior was required to complete a senior project, which included a section related to our post high school goals and aspirations. I did my future goals and aspiration section on being a collegiate level basketball player who was studying sports medicine. I did my research on which colleges offered that particular program. I also researched and reported beginning salaries for professional athletes, as well as occupations that use a degree in sports medicine. It all was right up my alley. All of my goals began and depended on my 12th grade year's performance on the basketball team. Nothing other than that ever crossed my mind. I didn't want to become a businesswoman, a lawyer, a doctor, an engineer, a teacher, or a police officer. I wanted to be a professional athlete, that was the plan.

The day had come. It was the last day of tryouts for the basketball team for that school year. The process was not new to me because I tried out for the team each year for 3 years straight. Everything went according to the workout schedule made by the head coach. We began outside, where we ran our timed mile hoping to make the time set by the coach, or to reach a new personal best. After running our timed mile, we went into the gym where we ran drills and scrimmaged with each other. This allowed the coaches to see how we functioned in game like situations. It also allowed the coaches to see our potential chemistry with future teammates. At the end of the try out day, the head coach conferenced with us as a group about the direction she was planning on taking the team that year. Her goal was to finally win the state championship with the varsity team and win district championship with the junior varsity team. She also gave encouraging words to those who may not make the team. She stated that this was not the end all be all and to continue to grow in the sport even if we did not make the school team. Coach, along with the rest of the staff left to go to the office to deliberate about the girls who made the team. She gave us the option of sticking around for 30 more minutes to wait for the announcement, or going home and checking the list in the morning before school began for the day. I stuck around for a while to chat it up with my teammates from previous years. While I was in the locker room, the head coach called for me to come to her office so she could speak with me in private. When I got in there, the other coaches all gave me stares of pity and sympathy. I had no idea what I was about to hear my coach say. Then she said very clearly and slowly, " Thank you for coming out for the team this year, but we aren't going to use you this year." In that moment, my heart sank. I couldn't believe she would have the nerve to cut me my senior of high school after I had been on the team for 3 years already. She went on and said how I was an excellent student with a great attitude. Coach spent the next 3 minutes telling me how good of a student athlete I was, but I couldn't get past the fact that despite all of these good things about me, she still didn't have a space on the team for me. I shook their hands, thanked them for the opportunity to try out, then I left the locker room and went home. I cried in the car, I cried myself to sleep that night, and several nights following. My entire existence in the high school world had some dependence on me playing ball. Basketball was my planned way to college. It was the only real goal I had set for myself. Any positive attributes I saw in myself were constructed around how I saw myself as an athlete. Nothing ever mattered to me as much as basketball mattered. I didn't know what I would do so close to time for decisions to be made about college and career.

I held bitter feelings toward ex teammates and my coaches for a while because I didn't understand why it had to be the way was. In my eyes, having to change the way I feel about myself, my goals and aspirations, was all someone else's fault. As a 17 year old girl, I didn't see it as an opportunity to seek out other passions or roads that would lead me to my initial goals. Several months later, I decided to attend college as an education major. I never really considered education until after being cut from the basketball team and joining a club at school where I learned about community service and other careers in service. As I grew older, I was mature enough to reflect back on my past life experiences and connect with the fact that education and helping children was also a passion of mine. When I was 21, I was asked by some classmates to participate in an intramural basketball team as a player for one team and a coach for another team. It was then when I realized that my life had come full circle in a way that I had not expected it to. I'd always loved basketball, but I never thought that I would ever play again. I began to believe that the purpose on my life was not to play professional basketball, but to fuse my passions for the game and for learning to become a coach and teacher of the game. That same fall, I visited the coach who cut me from the team. I was able to forgive her and get clarity on the situation. One thing she told me in our conversation was that after years and years of coaching, she is able to see when someone has greater potential than what they are giving themselves credit for. She said that I didn't need to be a player on that team to reach my goals in basketball and in life. My 21 year old self was able to see the purpose in getting cut as a blessing instead of an obstacle that kept me from what I wanted to do in life.

This experience is the sole event that shook my life up. I believe that the plans we have for ourselves, especially at a young age, aren't always how life turns out for us. It challenged my feelings as a teenager because I had to understand that I was not cut to attack my character or an attack my abilities, but it was an obstacle I had to go through to see my life for what it was purposed to be. It taught me the lesson that just because things don't go as planned, don't give up. Even though it took me years to see the significance in the experience, it allowed me to reflect on how rejection can be a blessing in disguise. It always reminds me of the quote, "A setback is a set up for a come back." Today, as a grown woman, teacher, and coach, I am able to frequently visit that coach who cut me. She is supportive of my journey as a basketball coach, and has offered to assist me with whatever I need as I continue coaching basketball. I will always remember that dreadful day of my senior year as a day that forever changed my perspective on life and paths to a purpose.

THE TESTIMONY

Revelation 12:11 They triumphed over him by the blood of the Lamb and by the word of their testimony; they did not love their lives so much as to shrink from death.

A couple weeks shy of the anniversary of the passing of my mother I was told, "Allyson, I think it'll be good for you to share your story with others. It's time for you to say something." I responded in a way to just brush it off like it was nothing. I am not a great public speaker, and I get nervous speaking in front of people. Yes, I am a teacher, but that is different than standing up with a mic speaking to others about my life. Especially my changed life that I hadn't adjusted to quite yet. But I trusted that this person wouldn't put me out there if she didn't feel I was ready, and especially not if it was God leading her, so I agreed to speak on what God had done for me and my faith.

I've learned in my journey to spiritual maturity that God deals with you on something and works it until He has you where He wants you. In this particular season, it was trust. I had become so self reliant that I did not trust anyone, and even had my doubts about what God could do for me. I was making money, I was buying whatever i wanted, I was well fed, I had a grip on my friendships, and I was traveling whenever and wherever I wanted to go. Everything was all good in world. When my sister passed, my life began a series of humbling experiences that forever changed the way I felt about God, and the way I lived my life.

I gave God control over my life when I was faced with emotion and circumstances that money couldn't fix, therefore I couldn't fix it myself. I asked God for a break. I was asking God daily why did He suddenly decide to make my life so difficult. I asked Him what He wanted from me. God responded to me and said, "Allyson, trust me, put your trust in me, and you will grow through and get through this." I said, "Okay, you got it."

There were times when I wanted to give up on God because I continued to experience test after test. If it wasn't one thing, it was another. I'd cry so much because I could not see what God was doing with this. I was still so hurt. I lost my sister, a close aunt, an uncle, and my mother. I was searching and figuring out who I was, I was in a financial crisis, work was exhausting, and couldn't catch a break in any aspect of my life. I would go back to God with my pain, fed up from suffering, in tears asking Him to help get through. He always reminded me that He has already blessed me even in the most difficult times. Even though the circumstances weren't ideal, I' was blessed with a new car and a home of my own. I was beginning to struggle financially, but I never missed a meal, always had gas in my car, had plenty of clothes to wear, and God kept blessing me regardless of my obstacles. I had to trust His will no matter what I was experiencing or felt. I had to trust that my breakthrough was not far.

I started to see that God used the loss of my sister and mother to get my attention. I learned to pray, to not only speak to God, but to listen as well. It cost me some things, some people, some habits, but the payoff was that God kept me and walked me through. He continues to walk me through because the journey is not over.

Through my loss, He has given me purpose, direction, confidence, strength, comfort, peace, wisdom, understanding, compassion, and fearlessness. My testimony is that God challenged me to trust Him with my life. I had to overcome toxic self reliance by surrendering my will to God and trusting Him because I could not heal myself.

FAITH

2 Corinthians 12:9-10 But he said to me, "My grace is sufficient for you, for my power is made perfect in weakness." Therefore I will boast all the more gladly about my weaknesses, so that Christ's power may rest on me. 10 That is why, for Christ's sake, I delight in weaknesses, in insults, in hardships, in persecutions, in difficulties. For when I am weak, then I am strong.

There was a point in time after I lost my mother when I felt like God didn't love me. I felt alone and frustrated. I felt like God was punishing me for something I did or didn't do. As far as faith went, I was ready to give up on God and believing all together. I had questions without answers. I had my life ahead of me without direction. I had a heart full of pain and did not believe I could be healed. I was losing way more than I was gaining. I was all messed up, and I couldn't see how my faith would or could change that. I'd prayed as best as I could. I'd cried on the floor of my bedroom night after night, asking God questions and not getting any answers to my questions. I was struggling. It's hard to believe things will get better while you are in the midst of turmoil. Especially, if you are going through something you've never gone through before, like losing a parent, or a sibling. For months, others were telling me that it would get better, I would see purpose in it all, and that I was on the cusp of a breakthrough. I listened and didn't object, but it didn't reassure me much. I was tired of listening to Christian people reciting scriptures to me and tell me that it was God's will, and all of the things they think are appropriate to say to someone who is grieving. The truth is it was all confusing me. I was fighting this battle of my human feelings versus my spiritual feelings. I wanted to rely on God. I wanted to trust Him and believe Him to be my peace and healer. However, I was also feeling like I was so far into this dark hole of being alone, pain, frustration, and exhaustion that God couldn't help me. But

I still went to church, I still spent time talking to those who I trusted to give me spiritual counsel, and physically I was drawing closer to those who were of the Christian faith. It was my way of trying to understand, for myself, how this faith walk works.

One late night while on vacation by the beach, I was praying, meditating, and just spending time in my thoughts. I began to read in the Bible about Paul's encounter with God in 2 Corinthians chapter 12, particularly verses 9 and 10. I found myself relating to Paul because, like him, I was at the end of my rope after feeling harassed by negative circumstance. What turned my faith, the thing that helped my unbelief, was God's reply to Paul's outcry to him. God responded by telling Paul that His grace was sufficient enough, and that His power is made great in our weakness. Those words, really resonated with me. First, it meant that no matter what I was going through, no matter how I was feeling, God's grace was all I needed to overcome. Second, it meant that no matter how weak I was, God was strong enough to give me the peace, love, grace, direction, and comfort that I needed at this time in my life. After God said those things to Paul, Paul replied by saying that he would look at his afflictions and circumstances differently because now he knows that his own weakness is God's full mature strength. That's what I needed in my life, God's full mature strength.

So, I chose to put my faith in God's grace and strength. I knew I couldn't do it on my own. I couldn't drink my way to healing, I couldn't find peace in not setting boundaries, I couldn't find love in people who weren't willing to understand where I was in my life, and I couldn't find direction for my future stuck in the past. It wasn't an immediate transformation, but at that time I committed myself to establishing my own faith, building my faith, and living in faith. I no longer wanted to go through the motions of being a Christian because of how I was raised. I wanted to actually live a Christian life of faith because of my own experiences. Over time, I still dealt with things I struggled with before. Me putting my faith in God didn't eliminate struggle for me. However, I was now graced with the ability to conquer my struggles, and I didn't have to do it alone. I began to spend my mornings before work reading devotionals and praying. I continued to align myself with people who shared faith and beliefs with me. I even began to fast for certain periods of times to seek God's will for my life and to focus on areas of my life that I needed help with. I came to learn in my journey that it was easy to give up, change my mind, and succumb to the dark places my circumstances led me to. I didn't want to be mad at God, and I didn't want to lose faith, but it was the easy way for me deal with my pain. I didn't do it alone, I had close family, friends, mentors, and even colleagues who helped me restore my faith in God after losing my sister and mother and after everything that happened afterwards.

Overcome means to succeed in dealing with something. I believe I overcame my season of unbelief by just trusting God's word, and changing my actions to line up with the faith I was building.

"*Dear God,*

Help me appreciate my weakness, help understand that all I need in my times of need and frustration is your grace to continue. Thank you Father for always picking up where we may fail, be hurt, frustrated, angry, depressed, and down. Thank you for being enough. Thank you for being the strength in our weakness. In Jesus' name, Amen."

- From a written prayer journal entry, 01/23/2018

THE JOURNEY

Isaiah 41:10 So do not fear, for I am with you; do not be dismayed, for I am your God. I will strengthen you and help you; I will uphold you with my righteous right hand.

Why do I fear September?
Should I?
What has the past done to me to make me dread a collective 30 days?
Am I still holding on to how for the last two years, maybe even 3, September has really been that bully who waits for me around the corner just to beat me up?...or down?
Is my anticipation for this season stemming from uncertainty?
Or certainty, that there's no way that September can ever work out
Because of all the ways it has left me scarred.
Are the things that remind me of September so bad that I wish I could fall asleep on August 31 at 11:59pm and wake up again on October 1st at midnight?
but wait.
September never comes alone.
It never beats me up, and leaves me be.
It has back up, who has also come to beat on me.
With reminders, memories, feelings, and emotions that are waiting in the shadows for their turn with me.

Why do I fear September when I've already won January through August?
Why am I afraid when I've fought this fight?
Why am I nervous when I've played this game?
Why do I hesitate when I've sang this song?
Why do I cry when I've been to this rodeo before?

I have the advantage.
For I've come to a time and place that I've never met, yet we are not complete strangers.
I know the moves and the obstacles I may face.

I am not fearful.
I am not afraid.
I can stand in the face of September with courage and not be defeated.
08/31/2017

I found myself at a stand still in emotion. Not because I didn't know where to go, but because I was full of fear. I had to pull myself aside to let myself know that it would be alright. I really got to a point where I was shuffling up ways to keep from going through stuff because I'd struggled so much, and I just needed a break. I knew something was coming. I tried to use fear as a way to not deal with something that hadn't even happened yet. How often do we do that in our lives? In that moment, I was writing my feelings of fear, hoping I could understand. I quickly realized that I had nothing to fear because my track record of making it through tough times was much more impressive than the history of tough times I've run into. There will be more times than one when I would I have to hype myself up, pep myself, and just encourage myself, and not allow myself to use fear to avoid moving forward. Fear had me at a stand still when I should've been moving forward. I overcame fear by understanding that I am made to handle whatever comes my way.

"... the next few months will be filled with memories. Memories that may bring sadness, some that will bring happiness, but what I want you to remember is that it's okay to cry, it's okay to not be okay, it's okay to isolate, it's okay to spend time in the floor, but know those are moments. Moments don't last forever, so be encouraged and know that God is with you always."

Excerpt from a letter to myself from 09/20/2017

SHINE

Matthew 5:16 In the same way, let your light shine before others, that they may see your good deeds and glorify your Father in heaven.

There comes a time in your life when the very thing that is inside of you is fighting it's way out. Sometimes it's an idea, sometimes it's a gift, sometimes it's a relationship, or sometimes it's word you need to speak. Whatever it is, it is ready to come out. I found myself fighting. I wasn't anyone else, I was fighting myself. I was fighting the things that were inside of me. I was fighting because I was insecure. I had these ideas, I had a dream, I had the plan ready and willing to execute. However, I still fought. I fought because I wanted to deliver perfection. Not knowing perfection does not exist. I fought because I wasn't sure of my experiences and my knowledge. I felt like my expertise was just to teach school and coach some basketball. I was selling myself short, and thinking small of myself.

In July of 2017, I attended a basketball camp for girls hosted by a mentor coach of mine. I was apprehensive about going because it was located on the other side of town, and I was tight on money to spend on gas. However, it was my passion, so I knew I could learn and also contribute. I scraped up money for the next few weeks, and drove from Lithonia to Stone Mountain to Atlanta for basketball practice. I also took with me a few of my former players, so they could get some off season exposure.

At the camp there was a coach , who was not too much older than me. She may have even been my age. As she was facilitating the drills and coaching the young ladies, I said to myself, "Man! I can do that!" I didn't say it in a manner that undermined her abilities as a coach, but I said it because I was inspired to bring myself up to the level she was proving she was on. So I took out my phone and began recording the coach, taking notes in my phone, and just fully becoming a student of what she was doing and saying. I felt the same way when other coaches came through the gym to work with the girls in the camp. I got home, I uploaded all the videos from the practices, videos from the scrimmage games, and any other footage I captured with my cell phone. I studied the videos, I studied my notes, then I got an idea. My idea was to do my own videos and create a YouTube channel to share my knowledge and passion with others. I wrote down my goals as far as doing this channel. Then, I searched and studied other coaches and trainers on YouTube, Twitter, Instagram, Facebook, and in person at games and scrimmages. I committed myself to learning, putting myself in the position of a student, in order to work at my goals. Later, I tried my hand a video editing in attempt to put a video together for my channel. After countless hours of watching footage, splits, cutting, pasting, copying, recording, deleting voice overs, music, and super dope transitions I was finally finished. Then I sat there. I scrolled Instagram, Twitter, and Facebook for hours. I had on my computer this work I spent many hours doing, and I found myself scared to share it with anyone who wasn't my inner circle. I'd already sent the video to my closest friends and family members. Their feedback was positive, but it was their opinions that worried me. They'd always tell the truth, but even if it had sucked, they'd support me in one way or another. It was the opinions of the hundreds of followers I had that worried me. I had known so many people who were doing amazing things of their own, and I felt I wasn't that amazing in comparison. The sacrifices I made, the people I met, the people I watched, the time I spent zoned out learning how to do coach things meant very little when I was staring fear in the face. Then the "what ifs" started flowing. What if nobody watches them? What if I get laughed at? What if I don't get the support I seek? What if I'm shooting too big because this is nothing new? What if I don't feel like ever doing it again? After a few hours passed, I said to myself, "So what, Ally? It doesn't matter what everyone else is doing. It doesn't matter what everyone else thinks. It doesn't matter that you do not have professionally made videos, and it doesn't matter if someone is better at this than you. All that matters is that this is in you, and you get it out." I remember having a conversation with a friend of mine telling me that I cannot control how others react, I can only put myself out there. I psyched myself up, and I did it! I put a couple finishing touches on my video, and I uploaded it to my YouTube channel. I shared it on my social media pages, I shared to my organization pages, and I sent the video link personally to several of my friends and associates. I did not expect to receive a lot of feedback, not even a lot of positive feedback. However, my expectations were exceeded. My video was viewed hundreds of times, had hundreds of likes between all shared platforms, and I was told that I did a good job. I was even told by a few people that they were looking forward to more videos by me. Over the course of six months, I made over fifteen videos and made eight of them available for public viewing and sharing.

    I was doing myself an injustice by not believing in myself, and comparing myself to others. This was toxic because although I saw others' success, I was uncertain of their behind the scenes experiences. For all I knew, they could've been fighting internally just like me. In this particular season in my life I learned to overcome fear, comparison, and uncertainty by focusing on my skills and just leaping. My light could not shine unless I realized that if I allowed insecurity to rule my actions, I would never be successful. There was something inside of me that was ready to come out. I fought it, but I could not win. As I made myself vulnerable, I created another way for me to live in my purpose. The videos weren't my initial thing, nor are they my final thing, but they are a ways for me to execute whatever my thing was to be. I learned that it is important to let your light shine so you can light the way for others. It is also important to let your light shine to light the rest of they way for yourself.

FORGIVENESS

"It's one of the greatest gifts you can give to yourself, to forgive. Forgive everybody."- Maya Angelou

In order for me to fully move on from the situation, I have to be honest about how I feel and how I was made to feel. I was scared. The thought of my loved ones not knowing where I was terrified me. The chance of me getting hurt or losing my life worried me. I have never been in serious trouble before, and here I was in handcuffs in the back of a police car. I had no control or say so, and that scared me. There was nothing I could do to change the situation at the time. I was embarrassed and ashamed. There I was a 27 year old, college educated, career having woman being locked up in jail like a common criminal. Not to say breaking the law has an identity, but I knew I had no business in an orange jumpsuit and tacky ass jail slides. I was embarrassed because I was experiencing the very thing I preach to my students and players about avoiding. The mistake I made was not knowing what I did not know. Everything stems from my emotional exhaustion that caused me to leave home in a haste. However, I don't want to place the blame on anyone else, even though they deserve it. At the end of the day, it was me who got arrested and had to sit in jail cold, scared, and hungry for 16 hours. I know there are some things that I could've and should've done differently, but I didn't. My financial situation really took a shift when I didn't get the funds to stay in school, thus not getting money that I was expecting to have. My first mistake with that was planning and living my life with money I did not have, and never got. As soon as I somewhat got back on my feet, I hit a deer and my car was damaged badly. A part of me wishes I would've waited to get my car fixed, but I would've ran the risk of injuring myself because the airbags didn't release. Getting my car fixed costed me $1000, and set me back in my monthly expenses. As a bill paying adult, I've learned which bills can hold off a little bit and which ones can't. So I thought. I knew I had to pay probation fees on the 15th, but I figured I could push it back to the 29th when I got paid next. I was so wrong. This was not a little bill that came with a grace period or a late fee, this was a fee that, along with a late payment came an arrest warrant and jail time. I didn't know. I hate that I keep making mistakes and learning hard lessons, but I'm trying to get to the point where I forgive myself, and allow myself some mercy and peace for the consequences as a result of my ignorance and immaturity in certain matters. I really wanted to blame someone else, and I could, but I just can't and have to take this loss for myself. The following Sunday after the incident of me going to jail, the pastor talked about lessons learned living on the margin. I believe my life these last two years have been nothing but me living on the edge. The edge of emotional frustration, the edge of financial frustration, the edge of not knowing which way to go, the edge of feeling lonely, the edge of insecurity, the edge of fear, the edge of love vs hate, the edge of holding on and letting go, the edge of belief and non belief. The lessons of thankfulness, self sufficiency, and being resourceful have all been hard lessons to learn while I'm going through these things. At the end of the service, we were called to the altar, and the thing that resonated with me immediately was when the pastor said, "Even though you are on this swing and on the edge, nothing is wrong with you. It's okay that you've made mistakes. God is not mad at you. He's teaching you a lesson." Those words and their meaning lifted a weight that had been on me way before I was arrested. It's hard to experience life when one thing after another keeps on happening. There were times I felt it was me who God was punishing for something I've done before. I felt ashamed of my ignorance and the decisions I've made out of my ignorance. I felt embarrassed of the mistakes I've made when I knew better, and just felt I brought all this struggle onto myself.

I had to overcome self forgiveness. This time in my life has allowed me to reflect on the intentional act of forgiveness. When speaking on forgiving, we often refer to forgiveness of others. However, I've noticed that we avoid the conversation or even task of forgiving ourselves. In reflection, I have realized that I've managed to forgive everyone else for how they have affected me, intentionally or not, but I've never forgiven myself for what I've done to myself. I think we owe it to ourselves to forgive ourselves in order to move on from things we take fault for. In my case, I needed to forgive myself for the mistakes I've made. I needed to forgive myself for not knowing better in some situations, and for knowing but not doing better in others. I shook myself from hurtful emotional burden that had the potential to sink me deep and eat me alive if I let it. Self forgiveness is important because it is the acknowledgement of being human, and not perfect. Allow forgiveness to liberate you, catapult you into moving forward while leaving the past in the past.

Overcome

Prayer has become a big part of my healing, and it's been an important contribution to how I've overcome the events and emotions of the past few years. I have learned that there are time where I just need to tune out the world and have a conversation with God.

In my moments of prayer, I have found direction, comfort and strength to keep living. It has not been easy, but prayer has given me reassurance that I would be okay.

I never thought of myself as a perfect prayer, but I soon realized that perfect prayer is just prayer that is sincere and from the heart. I began to fast and have moments of devotion in order to make sense of the things going on in my life. In those times, my prayers became more sincere. I felt like I was really connecting with God and hearing Him. I was always going through things, but prayer gave me the push to overcome. My life changed when I got serious about letting God hear my heart and me listening to His spirit.

Dear Father,

Please intervene on my behalf. I am overwhelmed with life and often want to give up. I have not given up because of you. Allow me to see what you have done already in times of feeling overwhelmed. Increase my faith Lord because I cannot do it on my own. Help me walk in to my purpose without feeling defeated so much. I know you will make a way as you have done before. I want to discern those things that need to be removed during the storm to lighten the ship. Help me see what is keeping me from you and causing no good to occur. Thank you God for your wisdom and faithfulness. Thank you for your word that gives us insight on what to do in our time of trouble. Draw me closer to your will and keep me safe as I know you will. Continue to encourage me with your word to live a life of proper rest and eating habits. I know I don't always do it because of time, but now I realize that improper rest and diet could be contributing to me having issues that may not even exist. Thank you for your encouraging words Lord and guide me to be like Elijah in finding rest and food first, so that the problem can be addressed with healthy and clear conscious. Give me the heart and the ear to hear your voice. Send your Holy Spirit to guide me through my difficult times. Give me the wisdom to listen within and not outside for your voice. Though the wind blows, the rocks, crumble, the fire burns and the earthquake shakes, I know your voice comes within. You are enough, your voice is enough, and all that you have given your children is enough. I know sometimes I say I want more, need more, but I do not need convincing because you have already shown yourself faithful in my life. Help my heart be content in my search for you oh Lord. Thank you for your Holy Spirit, Lord, with it I never feel alone. I can listen to the Holy Spirit within and through your people to get your word for my life and my situation. I love you and I am grateful to be yours.

I pray that you lift any emotions of frustration, anger, sadness, inadequacy, and anything that counteracts peace. I pray that you surround us with your love, wisdom, and protection. Allow us to see that days when we want to give up, you are right there to pick us up and push us along to better days. Give us the proper resources to deal with everyday life and its hardships. Bind the spirits of defeat in our lives. Help us carry the burdens that are placed upon us by others. Lay your hand on our hearts and comfort us when we feel like its too much. Give us the awareness that says take care of yourself before you take care of others. Lord, we know that all things are working for us, so help us in our faith to stick it out and see your will be done, Lord God. We know that when man lets us down, that you will never leave nor forsake us, so remind us to trust in you with our whole hearts. Keep those who encourage us around us and cause those with the spirit of discouragement to flee. Lord, heal and protect our families from hurt, harm, sickness, grief, or danger. Touch all of our hearts so we will learn to lean on you, and not man, for full comfort. Allow us to hear your voice louder than the voices of hate, anger, illness, isolation, confusion, lies, abuse, defeat, and anything that is not of your spirit. Rest on our hearts, Lord, so we feel relieved instead of troubled. Lord, we know that you can do all things that is why we come to you. We know that you will make our enemies our footstools. We know that you are our help. We know that you have made ways before and will do it again. We know that if we seek you first, that you will add unto our lives. We know that you are in control, so we give it all to you in this moment Lord. Hold us in your loving arms and keep our hearts, our minds, our words, and our spirits a God. We give you the glory, the honor, the praise, and all gratitude.

Father, thank you for helping us overcome. Amen.

Allyson M. Goode was born in Decatur, Georgia in 1990. She is an educator, an athletic coach, an entrepreneur, and a writer. Allyson has found purpose in encouraging, inspiring, and motivating others. She has experienced a great deal of ups and downs throughout her life. As a result, she has experienced forms of depression, loss of self confidence, overworking, and withdrawal from everyday life. With recent shifts in her life, she has taken to writing as a form of healing and growth. Allyson Goode believes that her story of overcoming will help someone who is going through what she has gone through before.

Made in the USA
Lexington, KY
04 December 2018